Adventure Story Bible
Book 23

The Greatest Commandments

Written by Anne de Graaf

Illustrated by José Pérez Montero

Bible Society

The Greatest Commandments

Contents — Matthew 18; Luke 9–11, 13–15, 17; John 7–11

Book 23 — Bible background. 3

LOVING PEOPLE

Forgive again 4
Followers sent out to teach and heal 5
The man who was healed 6
Saying "Thank you" 7

NEW TEACHING

The crowds are confused 9
Is Jesus the Messiah? 9
A second chance 10
The good Samaritan 12

LEARN FROM JESUS

Martha and Mary 15
The friend at midnight 15

WHAT IS BLINDNESS

Why is he blind? 16
Who was blind? 18

JESUS SAYS, "I AM..."

The good shepherd 20
Man or God? 22
Lazarus is dead 23
Lazarus is alive 25

GOD'S KINGDOM

To heal or not to heal 27
A narrow door, a great feast 27
Jesus heals again on the Sabbath 28
The dinner guests 28
How much does it cost? 30
God looks for us 30

Other Adventure Story Bible titles 32

Book 23 — Bible background

As Jesus travelled through Israel, healing and helping, more and more people were drawn to his teaching. Many did not know who he was. Many more did not want to know that Jesus was the Messiah — the person God had sent to help Israel, and bring the people close to him. But others listened to Jesus, and believed in what he said.

In all that he said and did, Jesus showed us a new way of living. It is in God's Kingdom, open to all who believe in Jesus and ask him to forgive them for their sins, then try to live in the way God wants them to.

There are two great commandments or instructions in God's Kingdom. The first is, "Love God with all your heart, with all your soul, with all your mind, and with all your strength." The second is, "Love your neighbour as you love yourself."

When Jesus told stories about how people should live, he was teaching about these commandments. Everything that Jesus did — from the way in which he brought one of his best friends back from death, to healing people on the Sabbath even though some religious leaders said he shouldn't — shows how important it is to love.

LOVING PEOPLE
Forgive again

Matthew 18.21–35

Jesus had been talking to his disciples about how they should love one another, and care for all people. Peter came to him and asked, "Lord, if someone does wrong to me over and over again, how many times should I forgive him? As many as seven times?"

Jesus looked at Peter. "Not seven times," he said. "Forgive him seventy times seven times." In other words, forgive and keep on forgiving.

Jesus was teaching Peter about what it is like in God's Kingdom. People are in God's Kingdom when they believe in what Jesus said and try to live in the way that God wants them to. God forgives people for all the wrong things they do, so it is only right that those wanting to live in his Kingdom should forgive each other in the same way. Jesus told Peter a story about God's Kingdom.

"There once was a king who wanted to have all the money owed to him by his servants. One servant owed the king hundreds of pounds, far more than he could ever afford to pay back. So the king ordered the servant to be sold, along with his wife and children and all that he had, in order to pay the debt.

"The servant fell on his knees before the king and begged, 'Just give me some time, and I promise I'll pay back everything!'

"The servant's debt was so great there was no way he could ever pay it back, even if the king were to let him try. This made it all the more gracious of the king when he told the servant that he did not have to repay him.

"So the king took a pen and crossed out of his book the huge amount which the servant had owed him. But then the servant went out and found a fellow-servant who, in turn, owed him money. But this was just a small sum compared to the incredible amount the first servant had owed — only a few pounds. 'Pay up, or else!' he yelled.

"The fellow-servant begged for some more time, but the first servant would not listen. He had him thrown into prison until he could pay back the money he owed.

"When news of the first servant's hard-heartedness reached the king, he was very angry. He called the servant to him.

" 'You wicked servant!' he said. 'I said you did not have to pay me back at all. You should have shown the same mercy to those who owed you money.' The king was furious, and sent the servant to jail to be punished until he had paid back the full amount he had owed the king."

Jesus told his disciples that the king was like his Father in heaven. He forgave the servant his debt, just as God forgives us no matter how much we have done wrong. In the same way he wants us to forgive each other.

Followers sent out to teach and heal

Luke 10.1-24

Jesus began to spend more and more time teaching his disciples and followers how they should preach and heal. He wanted them to teach others about God's Kingdom after he had gone.

Jesus chose seventy of his followers and sent them out in pairs. He told them to go into the towns and places ahead of him. He said that there were many people who would believe in Jesus and live as God wanted them to, following his teachings. But unless his followers decided to go and tell more people about Jesus, some would not even hear the good news he had brought.

Jesus gave these seventy men special directions, warning them that they did not have an easy job. "Don't carry any money with you, and don't waste any time along the way. Stay at the homes of good people. Be sure to spend your time talking about God's Kingdom and healing sick people.

"If any town doesn't listen to you, it will be judged by God. Those who refuse to believe in me are saying 'No' to God."

Later, when the seventy men returned, they were full of exciting stories. "Lord, even the people with evil spirits were healed when we gave them a command in your name!"

Jesus said to them, "Yes, it's good that you are doing miracles in my name. But it should make you even happier to know that you belong to God's Kingdom." Jesus was full of joy and gave thanks to his Father. His eyes were bright as he said, "Thank you, Father. You have shown these people your truth. Even though they are not the people with the most education, they have understood who I am and believed in me. And so they know that what I say about you is true." Then he turned to his disciples and said, "It should make you really happy to see the things that are happening now! The prophets and kings of the past would have loved to be here, to see sick people healed and the people believing in God."

The man who was healed

Luke 17.11–16

As Jesus travelled through a certain village, ten men with a dreadful skin disease stood waiting to meet him. They had heard that he might come that way, and hoped against hope that he might heal them.

Because they had this disease they were not allowed to stand near the road, so they called out from a distance, "Jesus! Teacher! Take pity on us!" They wore hoods over their heads and scarves across their faces. They were covered from head to toe, so that no one would have to look at their awful sores. They stretched out their cloaked arms, begging Jesus to heal them.

Jesus stopped on the road. His heart went out to them. They had no hope of leading normal lives. They could not live at home with their families and enjoy the everyday things of life which we often take for granted.

Jesus said to them, "Go and let the priests examine you." This was another way of telling the men that they were healed! When people recovered from this illness they were supposed to be examined by the priests. The priests would say special prayers, and everyone would know that the sick person was better.

The men did as Jesus told them. As they walked towards the Temple to see the priests, they felt a strange thing happen in their bodies. Blood tingled through their arms and legs. A strange warmth went up and down their backs. Their skin was actually getting better as they walked along!

One of them shouted, "Praise God! Praise the Lord God Almighty! I have been healed! I'm better!"

Then he turned around and, as fast as he could, he ran straight back to Jesus. He threw himself down at Jesus' feet and grabbed hold of them. "Thank you, oh, thank you!" he said. The man cried with joy, he was so happy, and filled with hope for the future.

Saying "Thank you"

Luke 17.17–19

The man who ran back to thank Jesus was a Samaritan. Samaritans were a nation who had lived separately from the Jews for hundreds of years.

Jesus looked at this man who had come back to thank him, and was praising God. He said, "But weren't there ten men who were healed? Where are the other nine? Is this foreigner the only man to thank God?"

Jesus was pleased with him for wanting to say thank you, and sad that the others had forgotten. Jesus said to him, "You can go and live a full life, now. Your faith has saved you and made you better."

Why did only one man go to Jesus and say "Thank you"? Maybe the others forgot for the same reasons that we might forget to thank God for the good things he gives us today.

NEW TEACHING
The crowds are confused

John 7.10-24

It was the time of the Jewish Festival of Shelters, rather like a Harvest Festival, and Jesus and his disciples were going to Jerusalem for it.

His brothers thought it would be a good idea for Jesus to go and get noticed at the festival, so that everyone would know that he was the Messiah. But Jesus said that it wasn't the right time for him to be noticed by everyone. He knew that the Jewish leaders there wanted to kill him, and that he had more to do before he died.

So Jesus sent his brothers and disciples on ahead, then he followed by himself. He entered the big city in secret, without anyone noticing him.

Everywhere he went, Jesus heard the crowds talking about him. "Where is Jesus?" they asked.

"I thought he would be here," the crowds said. "Have you heard of all the miracles he has done?"

"Who is this Jesus, anyway?" others said. "Have you seen him?"

"No. Have you?"

The crowds whispered and gossiped about all Jesus had been doing in the surrounding countryside. But the people were not the only ones looking for him. Some of the religious leaders who didn't like Jesus and what he was doing also wanted to find him. They didn't understand who he was and didn't like the

way the people followed him and listened to what he said. "He is too popular," they said to each other.

When Jerusalem was packed full of people, half way through the festival, Jesus went into the Temple and started teaching. "There he is!" A great shout went up as the crowds surged forward to hear him. With them came the religious leaders.

As Jesus taught, the religious leaders were amazed at his wisdom and said, "How does he know so much when he hasn't had any training?"

Jesus said, "I say what God tells me to. If you do what God wants you to, you will know that what I say is from him. I have come to show people what God is like, and bring them close to him, not to become a popular leader. So why are you trying to kill me?"

"Are you crazy?" the people said. "No one wants to kill you!" But Jesus looked straight at the religious leaders. He knew that they wanted him out of the way because he broke the Jewish Law. Jesus had healed people on the Sabbath day, when the Law said that he shouldn't have done. But Jesus said that the best law was to love one another, and so he healed people regardless of what day it was.

Is Jesus the Messiah?

John 7.25-53

Some of the crowd started whispering, "If the religious leaders want to kill Jesus, why are they letting him talk in public? Why don't they stop him?" Others said, "Maybe they know that he is the Messiah."

The crowd started talking about Jesus, wondering if he was the Messiah. Jesus knew what they were saying, and told them that he came from God, to teach what God wanted. Some of the crowd believed in him, but the religious leaders tried to arrest him.

The last day of the festival was the most important day, and Jerusalem was filled with people. Jesus stood up and said, "If you are thirsty, come to me and drink. I will give you life-giving water."

This water was the life which comes from believing in Jesus and doing what he says — a full life, doing what God wants, and knowing that he is with us.

When Jesus said this, many people believed in him, but others wanted to kill him. The religious leaders had sent some guards to arrest Jesus, but they were amazed by what Jesus said, so they left him alone. The religious leaders were cross with the guards and said, "Do you mean that you were fooled by what Jesus said, too? You are as bad as the crowd!"

But Nicodemus, a religious leader who had listened to Jesus and was interested in what Jesus said, questioned the other leaders. "Don't you think you should wait? It's against our Law to condemn someone without a trial."

The other men turned on him. "Whose side are you on? Look and see for yourself. The Scriptures don't say anything about a prophet coming from Galilee like Jesus does."

So the people were very confused, not knowing if Jesus was the Messiah. Even the guards of the religious leaders had been amazed by what Jesus said.

A second chance

John 8.1–11

The next day Jesus got up early, and walked to the Temple. It was a cool morning in Jerusalem as he walked through the streets. When Jesus entered the Temple, all the people gathered round him, so he sat down to teach them.

Just as Jesus started teaching, the religious leaders brought a woman over to him. She sobbed with fear as the men put her in front of Jesus.

"Teacher," they said, "this woman was found in bed with a man who was not her husband. The laws Moses gave us say we should throw rocks at her until she dies. What do you say?"

They wanted to test Jesus, to see if he would follow the religious laws. If he didn't, they would be able to accuse him of not following the laws given by God to Moses.

The woman did not even lift her head. She knew she had broken the law. The people around Jesus held their breath as they watched. He did not answer them. Instead, he bent down and wrote in the dust.

11

"Well?" the religious leaders asked. "What do you think we should do with her?"

Jesus straightened up and said to them, "Let the person who has never done anything wrong be the first to throw a rock at her." Then he stooped down and wrote in the dust again.

The people looked at each other. Each of them knew they had all done something wrong at some time or another. After all, nobody is perfect. So one by one, the people shuffled away, the older ones first, until they had all gone. No one said a word. In the end, Jesus was left alone with the woman. He straightened up and said to her, "Where are they? Isn't anyone left to throw a rock at you?"

She raised her head and looked around. "No one, Lord," she answered. She couldn't believe what had happened!

Jesus said, "Then I am not going to judge you for breaking the law, either. But make sure you never do this again."

This was certainly not what the woman expected when the religious leaders dragged her off. She went away, happy that she had been given a second chance to live.

The good Samaritan

Luke 10.25–37

One day while Jesus was teaching the people around him, a man who had spent many years studying God's law asked him, "Teacher, what must I do if I want to live for ever in God's Kingdom?"

Jesus answered, "What do the Scriptures say? Do you understand them?"

"They tell us to love God with all your heart, with all your soul, with all your mind, and with all your strength, and love everyone else as much as you love yourself," the man answered.

"You are right," said Jesus.
"But who are the others I should be loving? Who is my neighbour?" the man asked.

Jesus explained with this story. "There once was a man walking from Jerusalem to Jericho. He was alone and the road he followed was rocky, with many twists and turns. Suddenly, robbers jumped out and attacked the man! They beat him up and stole everything he had, even his clothes.

"The man lay on the side of the road, half dead. Along came a priest. When he saw the man, he was shocked. The man could barely raise his head to beg for help, but the priest only backed away and tried not to look. He crossed the road and got away from him as quickly as he could. 'I don't want to get involved,' he thought to himself.

"The man lay in the dust, moaning. Along came a religious leader, one who helped the priest with his duties. When he saw the man, all covered in blood and dust, he thought, 'He looks terrible. I don't want to touch him.' So this man passed him by as well.

"Then a Samaritan man came along the road. Even though the man who lay in the dust was a Jew, and Samaritans and Jews had been enemies for hundreds of years, the Samaritan came over to him. Very gently, he lifted the man's head and brushed the dust out of his mouth. He took some water and cleaned the man's eyes, and gave him something to drink. He put oil and wine on his wounds to clean them and to make them heal quickly. Then he carried the man and put him on to his donkey, and brought him into town.

"There, the Samaritan gave some money to an innkeeper and said, 'Put him in a clean bed and spend whatever you need to take good care of him until he is strong again. If it comes to more money, I will pay you the rest when I come back this way.' "

"Now tell me," Jesus asked, "which of these three men was a true neighbour to the man who was robbed?"

The expert in Jewish Law did not need to think very long before answering, "The one who helped him, of course."

So Jesus told him, "Then go and do just the same."

Those who heard Jesus tell this story knew which people Jesus wanted his followers to love. The "others" were not just friends. Jesus wanted his followers to love everybody, especially strangers and those in need.

LEARN FROM JESUS

Martha and Mary

Luke 10.38–42

As Jesus and his disciples were travelling around, they came to a village called Bethany. A woman called Martha welcomed them into her home. Martha lived with her sister, Mary.

Jesus was relaxing in the main room, talking to Mary, while Martha was making the house look nice, cooking, and cleaning.

"I want everything to be perfect," she thought. There was only one problem. Martha couldn't possibly do all that she wanted to do by herself. She rushed about, gathering herbs and vegetables from the garden, cleaning, and cooking.

When Martha paused to catch her breath, she realized that her sister, Mary, wasn't helping at all. Mary was sitting at Jesus' feet, listening to all that he said. "There is so much to do," Martha thought, "I wish Mary would help me instead of leaving me to do it all!"

Just then, Jesus looked up at Martha. He got up and crossed the room. "Lord," she said, "don't you care that my sister has left me to do all the work by myself? Please tell her to help me."

But Jesus answered, "Martha, Martha, you are worried and bothered about so many things. But only one thing is important at the moment. Mary knows that what I have to say is important, and has chosen to do the right thing by listening to me. That's a good thing, and she should carry on listening to me."

Martha was learning that it was good to work for Jesus, but even more important to spend time enjoying being with him and listening to him.

The friend at midnight

Luke 11.5–13

After Jesus left Bethany he went to yet another village to teach. He taught the people there about prayer and told them this story.

"There once was a man who came and knocked on his friend's door. It was midnight, and the door was locked as the family was already asleep.

"The man standing outside said, 'I need to borrow three loaves of bread. A friend has come a long way to visit me, but I haven't got any food!'

"His friend yelled back, 'Don't bother me about that! The door is shut and my family's already asleep. I can't get up and give you anything!' "

Then Jesus asked, "Well, what do you think happened? The man who needed the extra bread kept knocking on the door and shouting. Finally, his friend did open the door, but not only because he was a friend of the man who had called him. No, he opened the door because his friend would not stop knocking and had kept calling out to him."

People who pray to God, Jesus explained, are very much like the man who had stood outside his friend's house. "Keep asking," Jesus said, "and it will be given to you. Keep looking, and you will find. Keep knocking, and the door will be opened to you."

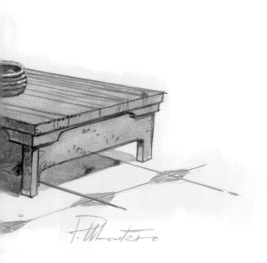

WHAT IS BLINDNESS?
Why is he blind?

John 9.1–23

One day, as Jesus was walking along, he saw a man who had never been able to see. This man had been born blind, and he had to beg for a living. As Jesus walked by, his disciples asked him if the man was blind because of something his parents had done wrong. Was the man's blindness a punishment from God?

Jesus shook his head and said, "No. This man's blindness has nothing to do with his sin or the sins of his parents. This has happened so that God's power can be seen in his life."

Then Jesus said, "While I am in the world, I am like light for the world."

He spat on the ground and made some mud. Then he put the mud over the blind man's eyes. "Now go and wash your eyes in the pool over there," he said to the blind man.

The blind man went and washed off the mud. "I can see! I can see!" he shouted. He ran to tell everyone and to look for Jesus, but he had already gone.

The people who had known the blind man from seeing him beg couldn't believe their eyes. "Is this really the same man who used to sit over there and beg?" they asked.

So the man himself said, "Yes, it's me!"

"Well, how is it that you can see now?" they asked. When the man told them what had happened, they asked, "Where is Jesus?"

"I don't know," he answered.

So the people took him to the religious leaders. Once again, many of them were cross when they heard what Jesus had done, because it was the Sabbath day. The Jewish Law said that it was wrong to work on this day, and the leaders thought that healing was working. But others believed that Jesus was a holy man, sent from God. "Who else could heal a man who was born blind?" they asked.

Then Jesus asked the people to think about what happened when one of their own children asked them for something. "Suppose one of your children asks his father for a fish. Would you give them a snake instead? Or if your child asked you for an egg to eat, would you give them a poisonous scorpion? Of course you wouldn't. So if you, who are a long way from perfect, know how to give your children good things, how much more will God, who is perfect in every way, give you the best of his gifts, his Holy Spirit, to guide your lives?"

Jesus was trying to show the people that his Father, God, loved them, and that they should never be afraid to pray to God. God will listen to our prayers, and knows what is best for us.

The religious leaders asked the man again about Jesus and what had happened. Then they said, "Maybe this man wasn't really born blind." So they called the man's parents, to find out if the man really had been blind all his life.

When his parents arrived the leaders asked, "Is this your son? You say he was born blind, so how is it that he can see now?" His parents said, "We know that he is our son, and that he was born blind, but we don't know how he has been cured. Ask him! He's old enough to answer for himself."

His parents were afraid to tell the religious leaders who had healed him, because the religious leaders had said that anyone who said that they believed Jesus was the Messiah would not be allowed to worship God in the synagogues — the places where Jews met to read the Scriptures, and to pray.

Who was blind?

John 9.24–41

The religious leaders called again for the man who had been blind. "Speak the truth now," they said to him, "we know that the man who cured you is a sinner."

"I don't know if he is a sinner or not," he said. "All I know is, I was blind and now I can see."

"But what did he do to you?" they said. "How did he make you better?"

"I told you! Weren't you listening?" the man said. "Do you want to hear the story again because you would like to become his disciples?"

This made the religious leaders very angry. "You might be that fellow's disciple, but we are Moses' disciples. We don't even know where Jesus came from, but we know that God spoke through Moses."

The man answered, "How strange that you don't know where Jesus comes from! No one has been able to heal a man who was born

blind, a man like me. You've always taught us that God hears those who do what he wants them to. This man must be from God, or he could do nothing."

The religious leaders did not want to hear that Jesus was from God. They were so angry, they told the man that he could never worship in the synagogue or live as a Jew again.

When Jesus heard what had happened, he went to find the man. "Do you believe in the Son of Man?" Jesus asked.

This was one of the many names Jesus used to show that he was the Messiah promised to the Jews. In the Scriptures the prophets had spoken of the Son of Man, or Messiah, who would rescue the Jews and show the way to God.

The man who had been blind answered "Tell me who he is, so that I can believe in him."

Jesus answered, "You have already seen him, and he is talking to you now."

The man knelt down in front of Jesus. "Yes, I believe in the Son of Man," he said.

Jesus said, "I came here so that those who are blind would see, and those who see could find out that really they're blind."

Some of the religious leaders who had been watching nearby said, "This is a strange thing for him to say."

"But we're not blind," they said to Jesus.

Jesus said, "It's because you think that you can see, that you're blind." This was Jesus' way of telling them that because their minds were closed, they had not been able to see him as the Messiah. But the blind man, whose mind was open, had seen Jesus for who he really was and believed in him.

JESUS SAYS, "I AM..."

The good shepherd

John 10.1–21

The blind man knew who Jesus was, but many others still wondered about him. So Jesus tried to tell the people who he was again, by using the story of a shepherd.

"The shepherd cares for his sheep and his sheep get to know him. They recognize his voice when he calls them and follow him home through the gate to the sheepfold. They won't follow anyone else because they know their shepherd's voice. Anyone who tries to get into the sheepfold by climbing in, instead of going through the gate with the shepherd, is a thief and a robber."

The people thought about this story and wondered what Jesus meant. So Jesus went on, "I am like a gate for the sheep." The shepherd stands at the gate to the sheepfold. He knows which sheep are his own and lets them pass through the gate.

"I am the good shepherd who does everything he can to take care of his sheep. He would even die to save them. Because the

sheep are his he does not run away when a wolf comes, leaving his sheep to be destroyed. That's what someone who is just hired for the job might do."

Jesus looked at the people around him. He wanted them to trust him. If they made the choice to follow him, then God would take care of them.

"I am the good shepherd. As God my Father knows me and I know God the Father, so I know my sheep and my sheep know me. And I am willing to die for them. This is something God commands me to do," Jesus said, "and I am willing to obey." Jesus said that there were also other sheep who, at this moment, did not belong to this sheepfold. He would bring them to him and they would choose to follow him. Then there would be one flock and one shepherd, Jesus.

Some of the people felt good when they heard Jesus say that, although they did not understand it all. But others did not like what he was saying. "What kind of person talks like he does?" they asked each other.

Some said, "He's mad, why do you listen to him?"

But others said, "These aren't the words of a crazy person. After all, he made a blind man see, remember?"

Man or God?

John 10.22–42

Jesus had tried to tell the religious leaders and the people more about himself. They knew that he had healed people, and he had told them how he was the good shepherd. Although some came to believe in him through what he did and his stories, many more doubted him, and others were confused.

Jesus was in Jerusalem again, to celebrate the Festival of the Dedication of the Temple. It was winter, and Jesus was walking in Solomon's porch in the Temple. The people gathered around Jesus and said, "How long are you going to keep us waiting to find out who you are? Tell us the plain truth. Are you the Messiah?"

Jesus answered them, "I have already told you, and you didn't believe me. Think of the miracles I have done in my Father's name. That should tell you who I am.

"You don't believe in me because you are not my sheep. My sheep hear my voice. I know them, and they follow me. My sheep will never die because I give them life which will never end. My Father has given them to me and no one can ever take them away. My Father and I are working together."

Some of the religious leaders and other people were so angry with Jesus for saying that he and God the Father were working together, they wanted to kill him there and then. They picked up rocks to throw at Jesus.

Before they could throw them at him, Jesus said, "Are you throwing rocks at me because I've made people better?"

"No!" they shouted, "it's because you, who are only a human being like us, want people to think you're God!"

According to Jewish Law, to pretend to be God was a very bad crime. The punishment was death.

"If I don't do the things my Father wants, then don't believe me," Jesus said. "But if I am doing what God wants, then even if you don't believe what I say, you should be able to see that I am doing God's work."

This was too much for many of the Jews. They tried to grab hold of Jesus and take him away, but he avoided them.

Lazarus is dead

John 11.1-28

Jesus left the city to get away from his enemies, and crossed the River Jordan so that he could teach the people there. While he was there he got a message from his friends, Mary and Martha, that their brother Lazarus was very ill. Jesus had made friends with Lazarus when he was staying with Martha and Mary in Bethany, and he loved them all very much much.

But when Jesus heard the message he said, "The final result of this illness will not be the death of Lazarus. Through it, people will grow closer to God."

Then Jesus did a very surprising thing. Instead of going straight to Bethany so that he could help Lazarus, he stayed where he was. After two days he said, "Let's go back to Judaea now."

Judaea is the southern part of Israel which includes both Jerusalem and Bethany. It was the same area where some of the crowd and religious leaders had tried to stone Jesus to death.

"But teacher!" his disciples said, "just a short time ago the people there were wanting to kill you. Why go back there now?"

"Our friend Lazarus has fallen asleep," Jesus said. "I want to go and wake him up again."

"But teacher," the disciples said, "if Lazarus is asleep, there's no reason for you to risk your life. He will wake up by himself."

Jesus said softly, "I meant that Lazarus is dead. I'm glad for your sake that we weren't there earlier, because now your trust in me will grow. Come on — let's go to him."

The disciples looked at each other. They didn't know what to think. One of them,

Thomas, said, "Let's go with him, even if we have to die with him!" They thought that Jesus was asking for trouble going back to the Jerusalem area so soon, but they followed Jesus to Bethany. When they arrived they discovered that Lazarus had died, as Jesus had said. In fact, he had been buried four days before.

Martha, meanwhile, had heard that Jesus was on his way, so she had gone to wait for him. When she saw him she said, "Lord, if you had been here, my brother would not have died. But even now I know that whatever you ask from God, he will give you."

Jesus told her that Lazarus would rise to life again. But Martha didn't understand what he meant. She said, "Yes, Lord, I know that we'll all live again at the end of the world."

Jesus said to her, "I am life, both now and after death." He was saying he was the one

who gave life to people when they died so they would live for ever with God.

Jesus not only gives life to those who have died — the life that he gives starts when anyone trusts in Jesus.

Jesus said, "The person who believes in me will never die. Do you believe this?"

"Yes, Lord," Martha answered. "I believe that you are the Messiah, the Son of God, the one we have been waiting for." She looked at Jesus, wondering why he had chosen not to come earlier. Then she went to get her sister Mary, who had stayed in the house.

Lazarus is alive

John 11.29–48

Martha slipped back into the crowded room. Her home was filled with friends, all mourning the death of Lazarus. She went over to where Mary was sitting and whispered into her ear, "The teacher is here, and he wants to see you."

Mary quickly got up and followed Martha. When she reached the place outside the village where Jesus was, she knelt at his feet. "Lord, if you had been here, my brother would not have died," she cried, wishing that Jesus had come sooner.

The friends of the family had followed Mary, thinking she was going to where Lazarus was buried. Everyone shouted and wailed, men and women alike. Lazarus had been a good man and his friends missed him very much. When Jesus saw them weeping his heart was touched, and he was deeply moved.

"Where have you buried him?" he asked. "Come and see," they answered. Jesus wept.

They led him to a cave with a large stone blocking the way. "Take the stone away," he told them.

Martha said, "But Lord, he's been dead four days, so there will be a bad smell!"

But Jesus said, "Remember, Martha. I said that if you believed, you would see what wonderful things God can do."

So they did as Jesus said, and took the stone away. Once the cave was opened, Jesus gave thanks to God. Then he shouted in a loud voice, "Lazarus, come out!"

Lazarus came out of the cave, covered with the bandages and cloths that dead bodies were wrapped in at that time. "Untie him and let him go," Jesus said.

Mary and Martha rushed forward, amazed at the thought that inside the white cloths their brother who they loved so much could be alive. When they had taken the cloths and bandages off him, the crowd cried out in amazement, and there was even more weeping than before. But this time it was tears of joy! Here was Lazarus, and he was alive!

GOD'S KINGDOM

To heal or not to heal

Luke 13.10–17

One Sabbath Jesus was teaching in a local synagogue. He noticed a woman there who could not stand up straight. She had been bent double for eighteen years.

Jesus called her over and said, "Woman, you are freed from your illness." Then he laid his hands upon her, and at once she was better!

She stood up straight for the first time in eighteen years. She felt like a new person, and full of happiness. "Thanks be to God!" she said. "Look at me, everyone! I can stand up straight!"

But the religious leaders were angry about what Jesus had done. They thought that because it was the Sabbath he should not have healed her. It was the same as working and no Jews were allowed to work on the day of rest.

Jesus told them that healing was not work. He too grew angry. "You hypocrites!" he said. "Any one of you would untie an ox or donkey and take it out to give it water on the Sabbath. Well, is this descendant of Abraham, one of God's own people, of less value than an ox? She should be helped, no matter what day of the week it is. She has been hunched up for

eighteen years. Why shouldn't she be set free on the Sabbath day?"

His answer made his enemies feel ashamed of what they had said. Meanwhile the people were rejoicing because of the wonderful things that Jesus was doing.

A narrow door, a great feast

Luke 13.22–30

Jesus was going from village to village and town to town, teaching wherever he went. At one place a person asked him if only a few people would live with God for ever.

In answer, Jesus told them a story.

"The way to true life with God which lasts for ever is like a narrow door — only those who do what God wants will be able to go in through it."

Jesus had once said that he was the door to life with God, and by listening to him and believing in him, people could go through that door.

"But once the owner of the house gets up and shuts the door, many will knock and shout, saying, 'Lord, let us in!'

"Then he will answer, 'But I don't know you or where you come from.'

"Some may say, 'Oh, but I knew you. I ate and drank with you when you taught in my town.' But that won't be good enough."

When a person follows Jesus, their whole way of life is different.

"People will come from all over the world," Jesus told them, "from east and west, and from north and south, and they will join together in God's Kingdom. It will be like a great feast." God's Kingdom is not for just one group of people.

And the order of who is most important in God's Kingdom is different from what you might expect. Usually, people who are rich, powerful, and famous come first. But Jesus said, "Now those who are last will be first, and those who are first will come last."

Jesus heals again on the Sabbath

Luke 14.1–6

The religious leaders who did not like Jesus watched him carefully, hoping to catch him making a mistake or breaking their laws again. The chance they were waiting for occurred on a Sabbath day, when Jews are not supposed to work. They knew Jesus healed people on the Sabbath, and were getting more and more cross about it.

Jesus had gone into the house of one of the Pharisees for a meal. This man was very important and he had invited many important guests to join him.

While he was there a sick man whose legs and arms were swollen up and bloated, came to Jesus.

Jesus asked the religious leaders, "Is it against the law to make sick people better on the Sabbath, or not?"

But they wouldn't answer him. So Jesus reached out to the sick man and healed him, then sent him on his way.

Jesus repeated the teaching he had given in the synagogue when he had healed the woman who could not stand up straight. That was on a Sabbath, too.

He said, "Which one of you has a son or an ox? If he fell into a well on a Sabbath, wouldn't you rush to pull him out as quickly as possible?"

Not one of them would answer Jesus' question. They all knew that they would save their son or their ox if they fell into a well. But to tell Jesus this would be the same as saying that Jesus was right to heal people on the Sabbath. Even though they knew he was right, the religious leaders found it hard to see beyond their rules and to start doing things differently.

The dinner guests

Luke 14.7–24

Then Jesus looked around at all the important people in that house. More guests were arriving all the time, and some of them were choosing the best places to sit. Knowing that many of them thought they were very important and powerful, Jesus told stories which showed who the important people really are in God's Kingdom.

"At a wedding feast, nobody takes the place of honour without being invited to sit there. If someone does sit there by mistake, the host might come and tell them to move down the table so a more important guest can take that place. No, it is better to take an unimportant place. That way the host can come and say, 'You are a good friend, come and sit in a better place.' "

Jesus reminded the people that in God's Kingdom people live as God wants them to. So the people who do as God says, listen to him, and love others are the important ones, not the people who think they are important but aren't doing what God wants.

Then Jesus told them another story.

"A man was giving a big feast and he invited many people. They were all people he knew and very important. But when it was time for the feast none of the guests turned up. Instead, they all made excuses.

"One said, 'I have just bought some new land and need to go and look at it!'

"Another said, 'I'm too busy! I've just bought some oxen and need to see if they work well together.'

"And still another said, 'I've just got married and need to spend more time with my wife.'

"When the servant who had been sent out to tell everyone that the feast was ready returned to his master, he told him, 'No one will come.'

"So the master told him, 'Go out into the streets, then. Bring the poor, the crippled, the lame, and the blind to the feast.'

Soon the servant returned and said, 'We have done what you said, sir, but there is still room for more.' So the master said, 'Go out to the country roads and lanes and ask people in. That way my house will be full. And I tell you, none of those who were invited will ever taste any of my food!' "

The first guests who were invited, the important people, could have come if they had wanted to, but they thought that other things were more important.

The people who really live in God's Kingdom are those who simply accept gratefully all the good things that God offers them.

29

How much does it cost?

Luke 14.25–33

Why did Jesus teach that it was not easy to follow him? Why did he say it was like entering through a narrow door and that not many people would find the way? Was it because it is too difficult to find the way?

No. It was because, like the important guests who were invited to a feast, some choose not to follow the way. Some choose not to follow Jesus because there are other things they would rather do. It seems as though Jesus is asking too much from them.

Jesus said, "If you come to me, you must love me more than anyone else.

"Before you decide to follow me, count the cost. Unless you are willing to live your life as I want you to — which means doing things which may be hard for you to do at times — you cannot be my disciple."

To follow Jesus means to be ready to do whatever he asks, and to obey him. It doesn't always mean that people must sell everything and leave their families in order to become his disciples. But it does mean that following Jesus must be more important to disciples than those good things — families and possessions — that they already have. Jesus loves his disciples and wants them to love him more than anything else.

God looks for us

Luke 15.1–10

Jesus may seem to ask a lot from those who follow him, but that's because every single person is worth a lot to God. God treasures every child, every man, and every woman. He would like nothing better than for each person to believe in him and love him.

Because the religious leaders were grumbling that Jesus welcomed tax collectors and bad people, he told stories about how much all people are worth to God. One story was about a lost sheep. Sheep were worth a lot of money in those days and were a valuable possession.

Jesus asked, "If you had a hundred sheep and lost one of them, what would you do? You would go looking for the one that was lost until you found it. And when you found that sheep you would carry it back to the flock, and call your friends together, saying, 'I have found the sheep which was lost!' You would be so happy, you would have a celebration!

"In the same way, God is happier when one person says to him, 'I'm sorry and will live as you want,' than he is when ninety-nine people think they are so good that they don't need him."

Another story was about a woman who had ten silver coins. One silver coin was worth a whole day's work. Jesus asked, "If a woman loses one of these silver coins, what will she do? She will light a lamp and sweep the house, looking under the bed and in the corners, hunting everywhere until she finds it.

"And when she has found it, she will call together her friends and say, 'Hooray! I've finally found the lost coin! Let's celebrate!'

"In the same way, I tell you," Jesus said, "the angels celebrate whenever one person says 'I'm sorry and will live as you want,' to God."

The people were amazed at what Jesus told them. It meant that all people, even if they have got lost and gone a long way from God, should return to God and his Kingdom.

Adventure Story Bible   Old Testament

Book 1 **In the Beginning**
Genesis 1—22

Book 2 **Brother Against Brother**
Genesis 23—41

Book 3 **The Years From Joseph to Moses**
Genesis 41—end; Exodus 1—11

Book 4 **Moses Leads the People**
Exodus 12—end; Deuteronomy 1; Leviticus

Book 5 **The Promised Land**
Numbers; Deuteronomy; Joshua 1—4

Book 6 **Soldiers of the Lord**
Joshua 5—end; Judges

Book 7 **Ruth, Job, and Hannah**
Ruth; Job; 1 Samuel 1—2

Book 8 **Friends and Enemies**
1 Samuel 2—20

Book 9 **From Outlaw to King**
1 Samuel 21—end;
Psalms 52, 59, 34, 142, 57, 23, 60;
2 Samuel 1—10; 1 Chronicles 11—12, 21—22; 2 Chronicles 3

Book 10 **The Fall of David**
2 Samuel 11—end; Psalms 32, 51, 3, 63, 18;
1 Kings 2; 1 Chronicles 11—12, 21—22;
2 Chronicles 3

Book 11   **True Wisdom**
1 Kings 1—4, 6—12; 1 Chronicles 22, 28—end; 2 Chronicles 1—11;
Psalm 72; Proverbs; Song of Solomon; Ecclesiastes

Book 12   **Working Wonders**
1 Kings 13—19, 21—end; 2 Kings 1—2, 9, 17; 2 Chronicles 12—14, 17—20

Book 13   **Elisha and Isaiah**
2 Kings 2, 4—9, 11, 13—14; 2 Chronicles 21—22, 25; 1 Kings 19; Isaiah 28—31; Amos

Book 14   **Micah, Joel, Jonah, and Isaiah**
Hosea; Isaiah 1—9, 36—end; Micah; Joel; Jonah; 2 Kings 15—20; 2 Chronicles 26—32; Psalm 46

Book 15   **Israel and Judah**
2 Kings 21—24; 2 Chronicles 33—36; Nahum; Zephaniah;
Jeremiah 1—2, 11—20, 26—28, 35—36, 45; Habakkuk; Psalm 73; Ezekiel 1—18

Book 16   **Daniel in Babylon**
2 Kings 24—end; 2 Chronicles 36; Jeremiah 24, 30—31, 37—40, 46—end; Ezekiel 24—32;
Isaiah 13—24, 40—43; Psalm 137; Lamentations; Obadiah; Daniel

Book 17   **The New Jerusalem**
Ezekiel 33—37, 40—48; Jeremiah 42—44; Isaiah 44—48; Ezra 1—4;
2 Chronicles 2, 36; Nehemiah 7; Esther

Book 18   **The Last Prophets**
Nehemiah 1—10, 12—end; Ezra 4—end; Haggai; Zechariah; Malachi; Isaiah 56—end

New Testament

Book 19   **The Early Years of Jesus**
Luke 1—5; Matthew 1—4, 14; Mark 1, 6; John 1—2

Book 20   **Healing Minds and Bodies**
John 2—5; Luke 4—7, 11; Mark 1—3, 11; Matthew 5—10, 12

Book 21   **Following the Messiah**
Matthew 8—14; Luke 7—9, 11—13; Mark 3—6

Book 22   **Jesus Touches People**
Matthew 14—18; Mark 6—9; Luke 9; John 6

Book 23   **The Greatest Commandments**
Matthew 18; Luke 9—11, 13—15, 17; John 7—11

Book 24   **Believing the Truth**
Luke 15—20; Matthew 19—22, 26; Mark 10—12, 14; John 12